EVENING MELODY

Printed in Canada by CanamBooks

ISBN 978-1-9990444-0-4

Editing by Su J. Sokol

Design: Associes libres design

EVENING MELODY

Rebel Bran

2019

Table of Cont ent s

TO YOU

EVENING MELODY   9

DRAGONFLIES   10

QUESTION   11

MOMENT   12

GIFT   13

SORRY   14

MY MYSTERY

SMILES   16

FIRST SONG   18

MY COLOUR

IN BLUE   20

1996   22

CHINESE GARDEN   23

HUNGER   24

JULY 28, 2015   25

WATER   26

RAINBOW   27

TODAY   28

DECISION   29

JOSHUA   30

JOSHUA'S DESERT   31

CACTI   32

SUN   33

NATURE   34

TELEPHONES   35

I DON'T KNOW   36

MY WHISPER

SIMEUNA   38

PRESENT   40

LUNATIC   41

2:06 AM   42

MY PASSION

TODA   44

4:15 PM   46

TO YOU

CLOUDS   48

O   50

BITS AND PIECES   52

COMPLETE SILENCE   53

ESCAPE   54

VEGAS   55

DARKNESS   56

HOW?   57

RAY   58

SEVDAH   59

RAIN   60

WISH   61

SORRENTO   62

TO THE INTERPRETER   63

KINK   64

MUTINY OF THE SOUL   65

~   66

MY DREAM

BETTER PART 68

INTRO TO THE SILENCE 71

THREE PICTURES OF SILENCE

   -X- 73

   -XX- 74

   -XXX- 78

FOURTH PICTURE OF SILENCE 80

MY PAST

UNDONE 87

ECLIPSE OF THE MOON 88

A CHILDHOOD MEMORY 89

^ 90

MORAVA VALLEY LOVE SONG 91

QUIESCENCE 92

DILEMMAS 93

WHITE SONG 94

BOREDOM 95

FLIGHT 96

HELPLESSNESS 97

DEFEAT 98

PLEASURE 99

VIEW 100

LETTER 101

UNCERTAINTY 102

VICTORY 103

GRIEF 104

TALK 105

OO 106

OOO 107

ATTEMPT 108

SALVATION 109

HELP 110

MIRROR 111

ETC. 112

BAD LUCK 113

QUO VADIS DOMINE 114

MORNING 115

XXX 116

VOID 117

I'LL GO 118

WACKY 119

MY DECEPTIVE LUCK 120

OPTIMISTIC 122

MY PRESENT

VIENNA WALTZ 124

TWILIGHT 126

ANARCHY 127

FEAR 128

MY SOUNDS

SEA 130

LOVE 131

BROKEN CAR 132

TOYOU

EVENING MELODY

It's quiet, a good quiet
not before the storm
not like a threat
Just good.

Like a quiet song from a Russian fairy tale
Pleasant to the heart
a bit sad but of the sadness
that soothes.
You know those silences?

Silvery shine
like the full moon in October
reflecting in your eye

It's quiet as your hair
before the pink sunrise
with my cheek
on your chest
like your unspoken words
that love

It's quiet like a comfortable silence
with a childhood friend
like the feeling of belonging
to the beauty
like among the tree trunks
of old-growth oaks
with your reflection
in the clear water
with no wind

It's quiet just as it should be
just like when I walk with purpose
next to you

DRAGONFLIES

Dragonflies make love on the fly.
In doubles, turquoise blue,
metallic argent, and silvery gray.

I wonder if love changes colours?

Flying cavalry in perfect harmony as one being.

Who is in charge if there is no charge?

On water over the water
Does anyone have to lead
or are they flying by celestial maps
printed on the water drops?

The fish.

The little fish.

In the abundance of algae and plankton.
They jump in and jump out, happy and sated.

How do fish make love?

QUESTION

What is this?

It seems familiar.
Scent of quince,
sound of major chords
on the piano.

It bridges over like a rainbow
under the Parisian blue clouds,
and feels like the relief that comes
after a summer downpour.

Why suddenly this peace inside,
and this strange, silly,
unexplainable smile?

I can't stop dreaming
and wasting time among the stars,
I have so many things on my list
but I don't care!

I stay in my bed
staring at the ceiling
completely exhilarated by its whiteness.

For hours!

All looks beautiful,
everything appears manageable,
all is singing!

Is this Love ???

MOMENT

Excuse me,
your hair is in mine
I say to myself
on the subway
when in fact I keep quiet
over a few
incomprehensible languages
Chinese I guess
probably Spanish
definitely Hindi
and a bit of Russian

Excuse me, again
your hair is too soft
for this moment
and this place
where every face
carries silence
under its eyelashes

"Excuse me,"
in the voice of a fragile
Japanese geisha
in a red coat,
resonates right in the middle of sounds

Has anyone seen
an umbrella?
In a hurry says
a gray-haired hippie
asking from one door
to the other,
then leaving

Excuse me,
your hair is still in mine
almost unbearably truthful
for this moment
cut out of the flying train

GIFT

I'm gifting you the lake
that I adopted
without asking.

I wrote your name on it
as big as I could
and now you are it.

I think
that under the thick ice
covered by the thicker white snow
its smile is friendly.

Maybe I'm wrong
but I believe I'm not.

Its waters and I
understand each other
as you and I do.

It must be perfect,
just like this harmony
under the azure sky.

Perfect as belonging
as certainty
as this belief.

As you.

SORRY

Sorry
is such a pathetic word.

Over-salted with remorse.
Over-sweetened with excuses.

Twilight is now
the colour of a ripe peach
and a perfect getaway
to the surreal.

I squirm with apologies
struggle with changes
reject confrontation
constantly
I cannot continue.

Instead I'm chasing
unmade-up scenes
and unspoken conversations
in situations unembraceable
that I do not want
and do not care
for any of it

for anything

for anything ...

I simply say that,
fighting my own thoughts
and feelings that I wish were
someone else's.

And yet, damn it,
I am sorry.
I'm so sorry
that I hurt your heart!

MY MYSTERY

SMILES

The lips are hanging
like a new moon
upside down.

Suspended smiles.

Following me everywhere,
conspicuously in my face.

A thorn in my eye.
A fly in my throat.
Pain in my knee.
Something in my loins.

The lip ends are pulling
down and down
and they can't go up.

I thought it's just me
the centennial,
but it's not.

The young lips
are pulling down too.

From lips to lips
checking everyone
till I only see lips.

Everyone, just everyone,
is smiling upside down.

I make an effort to lift the ends,
not even for a smile
just for the balance,
self-control even,
but it's hard to hold them
by invisible hooks
all day like that.
Eyes?

They can't seduce.

They reveal it all.

To everyone.

Like the overdone face across from me
trying too hard
but failing.

This image leaves a stamp in my memory
and again sends the lips
into the inverted new moon.

I hate glass.

And mirrors.

FIRST SONG

I have a kitten
She's crying all smitten
I give her a cookie
Still crying little rookie
I tell her: "Go away!"
She dances all day.

MY COLOUR

IN BLUE

In blue you painted
all the walls around you.

In that light blue colour
of the bluest sky.

And into that deep blue
of the magic hour.

In blue.

In blue you painted
the window frames,

the doors,
even the gutter.

The sides of the concrete stairway,
the fence, and the handrails.

In blue.

In blue you covered
the beds the sofas the armchairs,

even yourself,

in a blue bathrobe,

on a blue chair

on painted pavement.

Blue.

Everything radiated life,

optimism,

beauty,

care,

and happiness.

Everything but your tired eyes,

and abdomen that grew
with each minute passing,

relentlessly
sucking the life out of you.

Blue life,

which in despair
you tried to leave

on the blue walls.

But you left it in me.

For now.

1996 . . .

Some see where the water is,
but stone covers it.
They fear the black,
distrust the universe.

Water is drunk by the thirsty,
the sun evaporates the water.
The sky beautifies the sun,
and the sun outshines the moon.

This day in you
does it leave a trail
or do you go through it
not seeing it through?

Is this problem
overwhelming you
or does nothing
bother you at all?

Someone sees all is good,
the good is ridiculed by evil.
Someone hears about the truth,
but a second truth negates the first.

Someone sees I am smiling,
but it is a smile of sorrow.
Someone hears that I am speaking,
and what I say I'm not hearing.

This day in you
does it leave a trail
or do you go through it
not seeing it through?

Is this problem
overwhelming you
or does nothing
bother you at all?

CHINESE GARDEN

The floating stone
the water lily leaf that sleeps
the leaf that flickers
happy for the sun!

The water that is still
in the grass that caresses
the pine needle that I feel
from its peace to its touch!

Stone touched by the water
convex, concave,
soft and firm and careful.

Head housed by the wood
soothed and exhilarated
kind, beautiful, and ethereal.

HUNGER

Thick white fish
in an abundance of food
are downing unstoppably
chunks of current pleasure.

Insatiably unexplainably
frustrated
in perpetual
urge for satisfaction
they eat, swallow, slobber!

It's never enough.

The void inevitably
enlarges the dimensions,
as well as the hanging fat
stretching along the bottom

Hopelessly.

JULY 28, 2015

I'm screaming the conflict from within.
Always at the beginning of turmoil.
Getting to know you as a novelty
of a rowdy rock
and the forbidden heart.
I'm scared of losing you
and we have only just met.

WATER

Next to one's homeland's water
peace is most peaceful,
and the bluest.
Spirit is the cleanest
and breathes
a full breath.

Thoughts and ideas,
all the memories
and experiences
are in those molecules
and only there
do they feel at home.

Here, you're a part
of perfection,
not just a hunk
who never fits,
is an encumbrance.

Here everything works,
everything is known
without a word,
and it all makes sense.

Please

be my water

from now on....

RAINBOW

Today the rainbow appeared
in its most powerful colours.

Today is a day of joy.

Dogs play at the water's edge
in the grass that vibrates.

Full of life.

Under the sun.

In a murmur of friends.

I observe
from the blue-green armchair.

Am I here?

Where am I anyway?

By your side,

escaped

into the rainbow.

Without me.

TODAY

Today, I was lying on the dock
covered by the sky.
The depth of the blue
felt like
the universal spirit,
a part of your thoughts.

And then
they started
to emerge ...

dragonflies!

As light beings,
at an intersection with the rays of the sun,
one by one,
floating in the void.

Here and there,
here and there,
one goes
the other comes,
despite the wind.
Facing in the same direction,
at the same frequency of movement.

All
as crosses
made of light!

Your

.

.

.

Prayer

DECISION

As of today
I stop looking.
I don't beg,
I don't ask,
I don't want anything.

As of today
It doesn't matter
what I have
what I don't
I cleared everything out.

As of today
I refuse to look forward.
I'm melting the passions,
I'm drying out the tears,
I agree to run away.

As of today
I resonate with water.

I just am

as of today

with you.

JOSHUA

Joshua has lost his trees!

Along with the bag of magic.

They stopped along the way
for the Oracle.
Strategically grouped
among the cacti,
they hid behind their
chunky bodies,
with heads
that follow in sight.

They waited for us
just after Florence,
behind the last
widening of the road.

Under the sun,
buzzing
how they'll never
return to that
hedgehog
Joshua!

From now on
they'll just keep
the Biosphere 2.

JOSHUA'S DESERT

We met Joshua.

Without the tree!

He muttered
he misplaced it
somewhere behind the bed,
with the bag of Magic.

He turned
mumbling, I'm tired
of meeting those cursory beings
from the Instant World!
Those who just run,
glance and leave
and actually
don't see at all.
My desert
doesn't scream,
doesn't jump in your eyes.
It doesn't distract,
it doesn't glitter!

Snobs ...

For her you have to wait.
You have to
give her time,
have the attention,
and respect!
She bestows you with detail,
a slow walk,
breeze,
light,
and patience!
She needs to be seduced.

Honoured.

You low life…

CACTI

My cacti
from the sunroom
woke up today
without me.

I know that
the needles talked
as they do in the morning
to wake me up.

Then they waited for
the early morning dream
to Yuma.

And now here,
along the road,
I'm being followed
to the land of Palms.

As a forest
of cactus trees.

SUN

In a country
that locked up the sun
and keeps it for itself
just to spite everyone ...

Maybe only shares it
in small doses
based on merit,
or on a whim ...

Only sometimes.

When her appeal for
some green treetops,
some moist leaf
or curly roots!

Only then does that country
look over its shoulder
at the rest of the world
and close its eyes.

With a sigh

Shares a little.

NATURE

I must be
among the trees
among the leaves
to hide wrapped
in the forest
draped
in nature

Pour on smiles
give myself up to her grace
warm up with her peace
to sink and ferment
in her waters
in her hair
the sun and light

To b r e a t h

and b r e a t h

i n h a l e

and e x h a l e

fill with life

and beauty

And the beauty

of everything!

TELEPHONES

Restless and fatigued
heavy cloud
deaf, drab
too many people
escape the crowd

telephones telephones
telephones telephones

Like that nobody
should ever think again
Here but not here
touching
but non-existing
Chasing something
silent for nothing

telephones telephones
telephones telephones

Rain and drops
all over the wet
darkness and gloom
what does it mean
that door on a house
and lights in front?
Advertising neons
pawns, demons
devoured sayings

telephones telephones
telephones telephones

I DON'T KNOW

How many times my thoughts
go uphill with those words?

I'd like to know exactly
how much I don't know
so I know
how to start a day
with the right dose of stupidity.

This would give me a feeling
of knowing that I am
just a little bit smarter than yesterday.

This way I don't know
how to treat what I know.

And yet,
it seems that it's much better
not to know how much I don't know
because such people always
do much better
remaining in their ignorance.

MY WHISPER

SIMEUNA

Simeuna Hotomski
loves all her walls
alike!

They are whispering
stories from the past
and each has its own character.

One is a devil
one is an angel,
one is a dreamer,
another a rebel
and all are in fact
her mirrors!

Simeuna also
loves antiques.

And she's got a computer too.

She enjoys most the peace,
but in fact is
a real revolutionary!

She does not like injustice,
adores her kids,
and she is happy with the little things.

Simeuna Hotomski
knows that her walls
will never talk
behind her back.

That's why she feels free to enjoy
the old scales,
brass weights
coloured by smiles
and ancient anecdotes,
some escapades,
and invisible lessons of life.

And so Simeuna
does cry sometimes,
but she has no regrets.

All that she's seen and heard,
shared and taught
herself and others,
everything was with soul.

The way from the heart!

PRESENT

Turn
to your neighbour,
reach with your hand,
touch the closeness,
send a smile
over a distance
of estrangement.

Give,
share, flatter,
enrich, empower,
caress with humanity,
awash in tenderness,
say stop!

To look at,
to feel,
to understand,

it's a present
that you are across
my heart.

LUNATIC

It feels like
somewhere along the way
I lost track
or got stuck
some would say.

The values
The beliefs
Changed for the worse
And I find myself
Pulling
Grasping
Screaming!

The scariest thing is
Nobody seems to care
Nor realize
Everything is getting
Upside down!

And I stand here
Like a lunatic
In my own sanity!

2:06AM

Giving up Love
for sex...
Giving up Love
for sex...
Giving up Love
for sex...
Giving up Love
for sex...
Giving up Love
for sex...
Giving up Love
for sex...
Giving up Love
for sex...
That's the way
we go!

MY PASSION

TODA

The airport looks
like a Christmas tree,
or maybe
it's just my heart
fluttering....

Wheels roll hard,
powerful,
and maybe
it's just my hand
on your neck
that reminds you
that you are mine
in a way you love the most....

Now the whole town becomes
the Milky Way of stars
just like you sprinkling your seed
over your chest
when I'm inside you....

I fly
in my own manhood
you uncover in me again
like my suppressed alter ego.

The one that becomes you
when I mix my juices
inside you....

And I fly now in the dark,
on your broad
muscled back,
and with my kisses I turn
the lights of remote places on,
sprinkled under the airplane,
over your strong thighs
that shiver in ecstasy
as I penetrate you,
and over your round
and soft buttocks
that are begging me to take them,

to impregnate them,

deep....

Oh, how I would fly
with you,
often,
hard,
constantly....

Toda

Toda

Damelo todo!

4: 15 PM

Why does time drift
through my fingers like sand?

Why can it not be stopped,
caught, slowed down?

Why does it seem there was always
something better to do?

More meaningful,
fuller, more exciting, more spiritual,
more creative, more poetic,
more beautiful?

Only with you
I don't regret when time flies.

Ecstatic
in disappearance into your time
I know, wherever I go,
it does not matter when I get there,
no matter if it is completed or not.

The only thing that matters is
that it is with you....

TOYOU

CLOUDS

Clouds under me
Tiny clouds of plumule
Fluffy like the wool of lambs.

I love

I don't know what or why.

Oh, I love all that soft
Airy peaceful white with just a touch of grey.

I sing

inside me quietly but very heartfelt
spiritual the whitest softest
just like the tiny cloud
under me laid over as if it's going nowhere
and doesn't care.

I touch

All that softness like the top of the mountain
protruding through and teasing it
to watch over into the whiteness
but the impish clouds hand in hand
around the rock don't let go
they joke and turn and laugh!

I fly

through the blue air
over the red deserts,
down the hills and mountains
spilled over the trails of dry rivers
sand storms
rains that forgot the touch of white
bottoms of lakes
are turned into the clouds!

Where are my woods and groves?

As if someone has collected
the trunks in armfuls
and hidden them one by one in each cloud

separately

for me to harvest tree top by tree top
like white candy!

Where are my green lawns
to roll over them
with tiny clouds on my nose
behind my ears, in forelocks?

Someone gathered them in circles
like mom when she impresses rings
over soft dough
and a little here and a little there
through her fingers sprinkles the powder
from boxes full of clouds of sugar!

Clouds

Clouds under me

Tiny clouds of plumule
Fluffy like lamb's wool

I love

My tiny clouds

My mountains

My little skies!

O

This trip didn't have sound
It was muted like the hours
we were rolling
uphill

This ocean didn't have colour
It burned as words
we screwed up
meaninglessly

This silence was as heavy
as the inability
to get tucked
in the same ear

As if we weren't there
As if we weren't
within us

Melancholy of a die
in slow motion gyrations
as your intention
to take this road

Failed vibration
of our voices
broke up somewhere
over the naked cacti

Faces that don't smile
together nor separately
don't mirror
each other

Steps out of step
in between stones
without supports
fall in bleak darkness

I don't recall
if I was there
because your eyes
never caught my image

I lost your smile
in the downhill street
and I don't remember mine
so facelessly dumb

O

BITS AND PIECES

Wind curls the surface of the water
Mountains breathe blue
Clouds glide like foam

Dragonfly plays
with my bottle of water

It won't leave

Down the river
down a wave

Letters in the sand
34
Heart

COMPLETE SILENCE

This forest
is rooted
in lakes

My thoughts
anchored
between leaves

My heart
is counting waves
freed by the wind

I'm here
completely alone
fully committed
to this moment
place
sound

On mute

ESCAPE

Run away from mirrors
from my eyes
that do not follow the laughter
of mechanical lips.

I'm not here even as a shadow
that barely a few notice
only when
it covers their sun.

I'm not even sad
nor excited,
and I don't have any more
of those moments in me.

The time is out
of minutes
and the chest
without a grain of passion.

Steps do not leave prints
on sand
flowing away
with water.

VEGAS

Awaits
promise of fun
licentious happiness
fix of madness
pool of lust
moment of longing.

Awaits
the possibility of a smile
voyeuristic observations
no blame
no judgment
unawareness
and the Kingsized bed!

In a moment
I jump out of the machine
and turn into the me
I once knew.

I get to know
someone else
usually trapped
in a thick skin
of everyday
insignificance
awaken
by the moment
of possibility.

I breath
to grab
molecules of optimism
for the days
that inevitably
lurk.

DARKNESS

The power went out

All is dark
All is dark

Everything has gone
from hell to hell
but nobody wants
to ask any questions

If the past
was righteous

It took off
between a rock and a hard place

HOW?

So many people alone
so much loneliness
Heavy cheeks
Even paired
people are lonelier
than ever.

What is it that makes faces
stop shining?
What turns the beauty off?
What makes the soul age?

How do you forget
to love?
What turns
a touch to fear?
When do we stop still
in the intention?

How do we
forget
to love?

RAY

Ray
of softness
and freedom
launched
your hand
towards me,
opened your eyes
that radiate kindness,
spread your smile wide
that accepts me now,
softened the lips
that kiss me for the first time,
and say things
that make me ecstatic,
wondering,
elevating to the seventh heaven!

I can't believe,
but floating
in response
to just a small chance
of having what I've been dreaming
since I met you...

And that's enough.

SEVDAH

Where did you run away my pretty
So my eyes are not able to see you
Where did you disappear my darling
So my heart cannot ever find you

In your ever-so-gentle hand
you took away my dearest
So my soul falls out of love
and my touch rips it apart

RAIN

Sometimes
it's raining as hard
as life

No matter how many
clouds it empties
it's still heavy

Can't manage
to take all that moisture
and turn it into water

So it presses
washes rubs and drains
and drains away

Over the stains
that put up a good fight
but winning

Life is falling
Life is falling
The rain flows

WISH

And you just walk
with your face in front of your body
with a vision
that sees half shadows

And you are silent
in that muted walk
floating
in a strange neighbourhood
full of sentences
printed on cheeks

And all is flat
nothing whatsoever
skipping over your feelings
you forgot
in a semi-sunset
in hiding
behind the gutter

Yet
someone loves you

Happy birthday!

SORRENTO

Why am I so sad

by all this beauty

The lake

The crisp waters

The surreal thrill

of a time with a taken man

Alone

Again

TO THE INTERPRETER

Take me to. Translate me.
Take me over. Transfer me.
Trumpet me. Transform me.

Hearing meaning.

Take me in. Turn me over.
Transcribe me. Take me in.
Think me over. Touch me up.

Yes. You will
go on converting.

KINK

Be proud of your fetish
Kink
Kink is all you need

If you are not fucked
You are not normal

Uglify the beauty
Glorify cruelty

Imagine illusion
Realize perversion

Fantasize
Globalize
Ovulate
Masturbate

Be proud of your fetish
Kink
Kink is all you need

Say the right
Do the wrong

Wrong the good
Prong womanhood

Legalize what's illegal
belittle the regal

Fantasize
Globalize
Ovulate
Masturbate

Be proud of your fetish
Kink
Kink is all you need

MUTINY OF THE SOUL

Letters don't come anymore.

The real letters in envelopes
written with care,
with love for characters
and the person behind the paper.

Post has become made of silicon,
papers have become screens
and the people behind, faceless.

Worthless.

Like pixels that probably
don't even exist.

Time has turned into chaos.

The unrest is in the walls.

Impatience has become a nervous ocean.

Life's gotten crazy

and we have become the patients.

~

Skyscraper's top carries the sky
neon advertisements are nervous lights
one hundred and fifty metres off the ground
for twenty seconds of freedom in the wind
to bring me peace

Mafia by the neck
Terror of the battue
rage of telephones, guilty conscience
State security has a small task
freedom in the wind will end it all

Come on, come on
Come and look at what I see
Come on, come on
look what it's like to fly
look what it's like to fall

MY DREAM

BETTER PART

And while I was sleeping
my little friendly dream
dragged me by the hand
to an entirely different city

With not one street
with not one roof
on the windowless walls
with rooms without tables

There is no sound there
no leaf ever turns green
man of stone
long ago hid the smile

He took me on a long path
colourless and cold
his eyes looked mad

"Dreams are built by a good soul
that better part of the heart
with peace and strength
with a touch, a smile."

And while he talked
about all the grey in the dream
a bird voiced herself
a beautiful, colourful bird

On a maple leaf
a message cut short by her tears
she wrote with her heart
while dreaming this dream

I always forget
that I have no right
to destroy this city that's not mine
of which I have become a part
I recognized warm eyes
my luck
that's calling me

"Dreams are built by a good soul
that better part of the heart
with peace and strength
with a touch, a smile."

INTRO TO THE SILENCE

During the late 1980s and early 1990s, before I moved to Canada, in a Yugoslavia that was forcibly and agonizingly dismembered after Tito's death, and especially in Serbia that was primarily and unfairly blamed for all of it, life was lived in constant poverty and terrible fear.

The country was under severe sanctions by the international community, which led most people to the brink of starvation. Those who had a little money, trillions of useless dinars for a loaf of bread and a litre of milk, they waited in line from 4:00 AM to grab what they could before it sold out. Those who did not have even that, they were dependant on the government, who had been providing monthly supplies of food stamps for flour, rice, and potatoes, which was by no means enough.

My last paycheck as an urban planner, at the inflation of nearly 20,000 percent, was one Deutsche Mark. This was a perfect environment for corruption and degradation of every moral principle.

While the war raged in Bosnia, Serbia remained in relative peace, but the people had been living in constant fear of starvation, and the men, of conscription into the military. Most Serbs did not want to be part of that war, but the State had power to send any male to the trenches whenever it wanted, under threat of imprisonment and even execution for refusal. The abductions usually occurred at night when people were asleep. It was even more terrifying for many families in Yugoslavia who were from mixed marriages, fearing that they could be placed in a position of shooting at their own family! That was also the case for me as I have a (half) sister from Croatia.

In such circumstances the following four images of silence materialized....

THREE PICTURES OF SILENCE

-X-

When I wake up
these days I see a street and dead fish in the net;
I see something like myself
calling you through herds of headless roosters....
When I open my eyes
I can taste the garbage collection,
the tears are not tears,
nor is the touch what I expect.
The weight of my sleeping body remains under the blankets
and my heart is pounding somewhere like
balls striking the asphalt,
with blunt blows,
like a fist on a woman's back,
like rumpled hair,
like a quick glimpse of the legs that don't catch the bus.

Lame is the laughter that does not penetrate
even television pictures in squares through the space,
nor the monotonous sound of an air conditioner.
Shouts of children in the playground
these days bypass me in wide meanders,
and pointless profanities originated from my own stupidity hurt.
Castrated words can't pass through walls,
nor does my silence have any origin,
the thoughts are not thoughts,
nor pain.

Albino wanders in my circle,
and nothing around has colour.
The heads are dropping like leaves,
and the night is like the anxiety of empty halls.

-XX-

I'm taken somewhere by a road,
a way where nothing is assumed,
and doubt at every crossing.
I keep my spirit
listening to where the meaning of life is dwellng,
and always the same gloomy morning
arises in my mind
when I realize that, in the long line,
I'm stepping towards the bleary stream noise
as if I'm looking for beauty behind bars.

Years are hiding behind wrinkles and painted hair
sometimes in tight skins and expensive fake furs;
narrow shoulders and undeveloped bodies
are patched by sponge applications
and real wool.
The children ate all the teeth
and drained both breasts
after which only Dali-like sticks are left
to support time.

Every night such women look at me
behind the darkened windows at bedtime,
when paper planes stop flying,
so that, aroused by my youth,
they could be better for their flabby men.

Every night with big watery eyes
one pudgy, blushed-cheek woman welcomes me flirtatiously,
rushing to bed with her ex-husband
who she charges well for the illusion of family life.
And every morning a museum specimen
carries her urinal jar
to the toilet next to my bedroom,
writing with her head wrapped in a kerchief,
as slowly as the heavy silence,
that witches must be ninety years old!

Edges of my window and the tower line up
as I look towards the street,
and my apple juice drinks up a little more light from the sidewalks
to be spilled in my chest.

That way it's much easier keeping up with life
with a bunch of thermometres in pale butts,
from one to the other broken greeting card
for New Year's...

An indeterminate form of grief annoys me.

Simplicity is the art of ordinary souls
while I test even my swear words
and burden them by aesthetic analysis.
A thousand victories every day I take upon myself
to again realize how my faces are
insuppressible like water
and that one is always well-hidden
for a moment of surprise.
It's easier to unearth mutilated bodies
than dig into your own essence!

While planes glide down the invisible slopes
and intersected asphalt lanes guide silk cars,
a warm cup of coffee is waiting and I feel safe in peace.

That way it's easier to hold up till the end....

Melancholy and strength are mixing in the grey-blue sky
tied up in the treetop of the just-greened tree,
and when it thunders, I see rocks falling on the cymbals,
waiting for the lightning like a kid,
for without light even thoughts remain grey.

Night envelops me in darkness and in it,
on the stone breasts,
a figure of stars has leaned in.
In front of me a girl with golden hair covers my view
spilling water from the wooden bucket
as if she wants me to follow her trail.

Like every lie
the dreams like everything else have two meanings!

Sometimes my words in someone else's head
deciphers the code
and I find myself in the warm hands of a woman
that stings a thousand needles of lust into my pores.
Almost visible tendons and restless fingers
take me to the fields of pleasures
so I forget it will all be too quick
and melted in a couple of orgasms.

And when the moonlight spills over the sticky bodies
I often see some fly lost in time,
feeling the unpleasant tingling over my body hair....

That woman is sleeping beside me as many,
in essence untouched,
with no desire to touch me in essence.

What's worth the bird stealing a song on the fly
when she will still shit on just-pressed passersby
under planetrees?
What's worth living a rich life cheaply
when a gifted horseshoe might mean:
"Shoe up, you stupid mule!"

In the morning her laughter flows as it creeps
along several outdated scratches on my back,
and only the corroded contacts are left....
Days bring unsuccessful attempts to dig into the destinies
of strangers,
into the platonic women, and a constant maybe.

Maybe it is our purpose to search for comfort and excuses
but, after all, some dark residue remains that's hard to wash off.

Now I have doubts even of my own birth!

Moving shadows on muted ceilings
I watch from the street at three in the morning
as the breeze flickers behind my ear,
and the road always brings me to the colourful linings of the fair
that fade away in front of my very eyes
as empty bumper cars circle the floor....

Twilight always gets mixed up in my words
like grey flags in worn pebbles of dusty roads,
and with a heavy motion somehow I manage
to send a range of rainbow colours through the air
wishing to leave my hand marks on the rock!

-XXX-

Did you notice
how we're looking for motives
that make us adapted to death,
in order to take calmly the astonishment of the
curious crowd
who gossip about insignificant details
of our intimate life?

All of this is like the belief that in the eyes of my
dear wife
I'm the only real man,
when I could be anyone.
All of this is a consistently failed attempt by Marx
to create a new God through an utopian idea;
all is digging through the shit,
an illusion of business,
and feeling good through the failures of others.

Oh, how manly we take our women to parties,
oh, how humiliatingly feminine
they take us back home drunk.

In the absence of husk
the guitars are phallic symbols
in the hands of heavy metal sissies;
Dolls are replacing people
and people for every occasion have a different face.
Beautiful and unattainable perfect women
get on my nerves!

As the wine slips down my throat
my road is dragging to the fuzzy head,
to the memories of a boy's violin
in the glass cabinet of my parents' friends,
to the envy of children from the dormitory
satisfied with just sneakers, a jacket and pants,
to the hope that up there won't wait for me
an ordeal in exchange for remorse.

FOURTH PICTURE OF SILENCE

"It's been a while since I had ..."
said a man
filling up with caramel coloured liquid.
"It's the only way,
through a heavy volume of smoke,
to unlock my secrets by verbal torture!"

"Quite by accident, you are now here
as another unknown face in a sea,
suspiciously curious about listening
another even less known.

This will be my barren shedding
of love for humanity, anyway!

Just save me from bad luck and envy,
happiness and failure,
when happiness comes more from other people's grief.

The most important thing is whether it is good weather!

Too often you go back to romantic exploits
when the only thing remaining
is the one who refused to lay,
like that something to always desire.

That you know.

And when you wake up, you realize that for centuries
you run after the one without name!

A man is defined by a woman,
and a woman by her husband,
at the edge of the eroticized half-hour
and grey, dry, square lust,
always on the verge of buying and selling feelings.

And between two humiliating quarrels,
or a resigned overpass,
you squeeze through mistakes
in trying to avoid ugliness and bitterness,
sarcasm and hypocrisy,
asking for God, sure of your paganism.

She preens, fixes her hair, face powder
for tonight's party,
expecting the most normal understanding of freedom,
because this is the time of emancipation,
in which women show their true strength
hiding their faces behind colourful make up.

So you try extremely hard
to impress the impression,
with a few words you eroticize the mood,
and half-jokingly you toy with
the biggest truth you believe in:
your brains are in vain if you don't fuck well!

Through the blankets and underwear you deduce
that with age remains the need for sucking
for both sexes.

This is a dedicated lay,
everyone here is waiting for their own orgasm.

If she wants more, no worries,
you'll let others fuck in Technicolor,
and the scene will again be potent!

At the end, put up some drama for the facade,
that's life,
and then you go back to your separate beds
to your apathetic families.

Tonight again they kill stray dogs around town,
and I would trade it all for a tiny piece of beauty,
I wouldn't worry others to stop worrying myself;
I'd run away from permanent self-confirmation
when corroboration from others is decreasingly less;
from identifying with your idols,
from pondering life
that inevitably leads to death....

Trendily you become the ecologist of your own soul
buying yourself presents with cards for birthdays,
toasting by yourself and your always-ready
guardians of your sunken ships.

Running away from pathetic love poetry
that you see then like long-drawn food scraps
you are always surprised
by mini-minded people and their
monumental nonsense!

You shorten your memory
so there is less pain from the insane parties
of hilarious groups of past friends,
now rejoicing in ncreasingly rare mindless conversations,
when the others are nonexistent.

I'm talking about small truths
on the other side of the mask,
behind the views that don't actually see,
paying attention to different tones of applause
wondering why are just these people around me?

The same ones who don't notice,
or even worse, dispute,
building your fortress of self-sufficiency,
impelling you to look only at yourself
to find an oasis there,
to get between two strikes of a church bell,
into a bohemian song
burned out in the street and alcohol,
to see how the seashell walk,
and every day you overcome yourself
in hunting for meaningful perspectives
on which you can rely.

At twenty-five you start to live from memories
aware of your molten charm,
and you are only sure of your new tangible wrinkles.
How could you not,
when ideas are decaying overnight,
when we define how we will feel tomorrow,
and when nature only remains on projections?

In an instant you are, again, full of optimism and faith,
all glands are working fine,
and you are happy to wait for old age.
And then some kind of warning
switches back the suspicion,
and all floats away like a balloon.

Then again you take all the surrounding worries,
whilst fearing for your hands and your thoughts
you feel unbearable weight in your joints,
brain mass and critical fullness of your scull.

You switch all the blame to Turks
and so falls your view of yourself,
so when you don't have yourself,
you turn to imitation and let yourself be
just an image of destiny.

Then what letters do not come don't matter,
nor fear of neighbours
who would have you sent to the mental hospital,
and it hardly hurts even thinking of former comrades
who hung themselves!

You let yourself go to the world of hits and fashion,
small, useful lies,
and you protect your nerves from compromising.

You try to feel the touch by teeth,
and do bollocks just for fun
craving to tear the bread in half at the Stonehenge
and devour it with bacon!
Completely insane, because when you are buying bread
you always think about toilet paper too!

Maybe enlightenment passes by
without us being aware of it.

Maybe it's better
we get away from the human dimension!"

MY PAST

UNDONE

I saw you under the Moon
unlocked
liberated
soft
absorbing the light
through your tender skin.

I saw you curl up
like a wave slowly but firmly
loving your body
and all your trembles for me,
letting me savour you
with my eyes.

And I've seen you no longer running scared,
safe from your past
and sure about your future.

Your eyes are glowing
while you're feeling
what leaves are feeling under the wind,
what land hears when grass flourishes,
your breasts are alert
in self-awareness bathed in moonlight
in which I saw you
in your unrestrained
unlocked
unsanctioned
wish to discover
a man in me,
to make him....

Tonight I breathed you again
for the first time free and yours
before the dismantled cage
you threw away behind the shadow,
bathed in sliver,
soft,
seducing,
you touched my shoulder with your cheek
and felt me....

ECLIPSE OF THE MOON

The moon is being eaten up by my planet
A silvery spider web of fog
spread between the treetops is silent
The fields like ribbons
are racing before my face
I am full to the brim with stars...

A CHILDHOOD MEMORY

Winter time again has cast a thin foil over the road
like sugar and water when they get dry….
You know,
when over the snow she spits the rain
then deep freezes it.

The salt is eating away my shoes
I need new ones
but they are too pricey,
for the bigger they are the pricier they get.
45….

Afternoon.
My room awashed in daylight.
Day slipping down the slope on the opposite side.
I catch the last ray....

MORAVA VALLEY LOVE SONG

I'm breathing in your soul
from the winds of Morava Valley,
and with your hair brought by
the winter snow
I bind my heart into golden braids
to soothe the beat
turning into echoes ....

Quiet
in the shadow of the clouds that smother,
staring into the endless void
only with you in my sight,
and love ascending from the waters.

How many moments are needed
to turn into time?
How many dusks are needed
to comprehend the value of life?

QUIESCENCE

For days I keep quiet.
For days not a word I want to say.
I read my poems out loud
to remember my voice.
I step into the heat of my passion
that obscures the view with a warm vapour.

36 in the shade,
hell ...
Naked on the bed
I blow another butterfly
and persistently masturbate my brain.

DILEMMAS

Between my different selves in the glass,
in the polygon of lines is my face,
halfway upon it is the shadow,
from halfway up is sight
and a finger pointing to the eye.

Is everything I see colour
and all I hear word?
Do you exist kissing me
or am I only in your dream?

WHITE SONG

Sucked in dust
between the stones on the road
I look at
a glass window in the sky
and white curtains.

I watch the soles of beings in white.
They march out without faces there,
two feet above the road
and three under the window.

One after another
One by one
like one

White road, bare white foot,
white patch across the white body.

A mosque or a church stretched its tower
to break the sky hymen,
because,
children will come from God
so kiss your Madonna
and walk in white....

One after another
One by one
and look up!
At the top of the tower is stereo,
20 meters of tape and voice:
"Walk, walk,
a wooden scaffold is the goal."

While you're going down you fade away,
you'll be white as a white patch!
You are a rag,
you are nothing,
white....

BOREDOM

Nothing is happening at all.
If someone at least
would twist a faulty faucet
it seems again
the patina of day
would take over for the night....

Or if the second chair
would be taken by you
I wouldn't fear for mine.

This way, only my weight
would leave an impression upon it.

FLIGHT

Little girl's breasts
got cold.

The boy was running
looking at the silver plane
lying upon
the crumbling roof tile
above his small bedroom.

He reaches out and his eyes spark,
he opens the small door,
walks through the narrow aisles,
sits.

Before him a courtyard
like sky on his palm, teasing.

He flies around kitty's tail,
about grandpa's cherry,
around cotton candy,
from cloud to cloud,
stretched out bare little arms,
and happy, wide open eyes.

HELPLESSNESS

Silence of darkness
falling as a leaf
on my relaxed shoulders;
I cut the silence
like a million heads raised;
how to deny the truth
falling out from torn bags?

DEFEAT

A rough hand catches the goodness
spilled out in a swing
creating a heap of paper
as a gift to the wind.
I kept quiet
dumb....

PLEASURE

To start,
start, commence, beget,
embryo of my suppressed
passions.
In a hand a flower is blooming
with peeled petals,
and eyes, what they can do
except to see and to hurt?
It's a long way for spermatozoid,
but short-lived is the empty pleasure.

VIEW

grain   and grain   of sand
   and grain   grain   of sand
      on skin   in   pores
    almost   invisible   I touch
at the   proper   distance
   with drops   of sweat   from   the sun
      like   dewdrops
   from hands   the view   slips
    over   every   rock   and grain
by grain   of sand   to the water
    over   the line
    behind which   the sun   sets

LETTER

it's satisfying to slap a hand
on calm water puddles,
on blood with alcohol,
in concentric circles
of grief....

UNCERTAINTY

Crystals
as sharp as an insult
are everywhere,
pain
dull and enduring
over it all as a dark cloak,
the universe
as nothing,
as something where salvation grows....

VICTORY

You walk breached by the swelter
of my words.
With conscience torn up by a bundle
of dull nails
I won
another pawn.

GRIEF

A tiny green valley
bounced
into my mouth
melted with laughter.

TALK

Words like knotted balls
roll along the wires,
then when preparing text
for three previous days
so it chokes your throat and you hear:
        how is it going
        good
        well
        maybe
        no
and the only thing you have left is to stretch
your arm
and flush it.

Silence is too long,
the handset is swinging in the wind
I miss you
cuts deep into space
but not enough
to reach your ear….

●●

Alone Alone Alone
as a bite thrown through
the window of the car
as a cripple, and as crazy

• • •

A long time
A long time I haven't
Too long nothing have I
Written
To anybody
A long time already

ATTEMPT

Through a wrecked gutter
thought is clinking cruising
to a distant star pointed down.
On the other side
I'm trying to push through a look
but new light meets me.
I loosen my belt to bend more
watching through rows of eyelashes
clenched eyelids
but it hurts.
No way to think.

SALVATION

Run, even dive
under your own crust,
take your skin off the horns
stabbed deep beneath the udder,
rescue yourself from the sludge
cunt!

HELP

Step a little harder
over the red river,
Ma!
The rain is collapsing,
I wandered off
and I don't know.
Pass the small finger
of straw at least.

MIRROR

In each round there is
one of these and one of those
like points.
With a few drops
of red or white wine
the points disperse
but within their limits.
Everyone is someone
as one and only
right along.

ETC.

A tobacco coloured cube
is falling towards the nebula of the lungs
in slow motion
and bursts.
On the blue cut
wrinkles are drawing my face.

I put it out
and light it up again
etc.

BAD LUCK

I know that behind, deep traces remain.
The snow is again soft and white
and glows like the white night sky.
I'm not looking,
but ahead is a woman like you,
like you, God,
to touch the feet floating behind the line....

For a moment I'm there
looking at her sleeping weightless
a metre above the snow,
on my palm
that's trembling with fear and passion
melting her.

Every touch
turns her into a body of water,
and I hear from the last outline,
through the glance of pity:
"You are too hot, boy,
you've got a fever..."

QUO VADIS DOMINE

The world is falling
on the land that does not hold it.

MORNING

I get up and look
at the wrinkled night under me.
I dreamed of nothing
but bed is like a war zone.
As the emptiness
is angrier than dreams....

XXX

Russian girl
shows off her breasts
and below...
"Grandpa,
look at your happiness!"

VOID

This nothing in between is tormenting….
I'm left hanging
with no legs and no soil underneath.
Bird without beak
with no feathers
and one broken wing.
Falsetto.

I ' LL GO

I'll draw a line,
I'll take the ends
to wrap around my neck,
and tighten it as hard as I can.

I'll grab my hair
and put myself through the knot,
take off my shirt,
show my chest to people
and shout
like a voiceless face
with open mouth
and strained veins on my neck.

As always so far
in vain.
Nothing else left
but to wipe myself away with an eraser!

WACKY

A little green house
has fallen from Mars
once
when with a trolley
I jumped on asphalt,
like mad, like an elevator,
up and down up and down
up down
up
down
u
d
u
.
.
.

MY DECEPTIVE LUCK

The dish I'm flying on
is not comfy at all
but I fly,
blinded by the illusion of speed
when all forms turn into
parallel lines,
like expressive strokes
of an artist in ecstasy.

Someone from the surface is throwing stones....

Stone by stone they submerge,
and then like they're zonked,
in a curved line descend to the bottom.

In passing I swallow any residual bubbles
from the air up there,
it will be enough for the next day
to kill the dragonfish by oxygen....

Under water the flames of my endless uneasiness
are burning.

Every night I go up in the dark,
on the hill of Eden I've got my world
of a square metre,
and I see it all beautifully.

It's dark
and I do not feel the wounds.
The moon is silent
and we understand each other without saying anything.

Before the morning I step with bare feet
in cold ink
that stirs up my blood.
I'm afraid of wasting another day
till the next night
and the moon.

OPTIMISTIC

Pictures are furling on their own.

A massive snore of deadened soldiers
on the rampage called crisis,
in the darkness of the room,
through a narrow slit in the door
while a light beam is sliding along the ceiling....

Face exhausted by sadness
with the bags of drinking under the eyes.

Flooding everywhere from North to South.

My train is rattling along the tracks
freezing its wheels
by the porridge of spilled dirt
that leaks and leaks,
and I, mesmerized by the image,
love the boy from the riverside
who just like that,
out of pure emotion,
raises his arm,
and waves, waves,
happy....

MY PRESENT

VIENNA WALTZ

I'm assured,
it doesn't suit just the Danube:
it suits every body of water.

A colourful coffee shop on the stripes
welcomes me in yellow and mocha.

Lemon and coffee and a bottle of beer
on a round table on the stripes,
yellow and mocha,
what am I saying?

Of course,
a scorpion went
right by my right hand.

Chairs and table
were nailed to the concrete.

How stupid is that!

But it was nice to see
twenty round tables
on the stripes,
and Strauss' Vienna Waltz.

And seaweed,
mocha-coloured,
strange,
mocha like the stripes in the cafe.

And then the table on the stripes
raised by my nose
and in slow motion
flew into the sea like a butterfly
to the beat

one two three

two two three

one two three

two two three

and me with it.

I didn't even know that The Vienna Waltz
isn't only for the Danube...

TWILIGHT

Icicles were falling from the gutters
under the struggling midday winter sun,
and around five
I slapped it with both hands
to relax its biceps,
when I saw
how it blushes to purple,
sliding along the parapet
of the big white building.

There it starts the game of movement
corner, edge, edge, corner,
corner, edge, rim,
and a long flight
down the drapes of the sky,
to the bottom of the ice....

Like a cent
in the slot of the piggy bank
it hid behind
till morning....

ANARCHY

Power without authority
  tear from the urge
    red-hot consciousness
      above the asphalt road
      under the summer sun

Glass in the grass
  brown from snow,
    crushed by the hand of anger

A car with no roof
  on the left side of the road
    and a passenger without a head
      scattered blood over the seats

FEAR

In total despoilment I grab
from long longer
from big bigger
grab from bigger more
I grab the grab.
I carve it word by word on the skin,
With thoughts I think the thoughts,
I don't want to die old,
nor young....

MY SOUNDS

SEA

Fishimimi siolini
dirliminini sishi
oooooo malanuva fuva
dulava vulada butch

A dana salana gala
mufila usnila gui
sushima tchutchuna glama
bertch trutch

LOVE

Auvioa moaiani aa
ooonihanimai vuini mia
moni
moni oliavidaao
oliavidaao moni hai

Haliminaivio dalismaani
haliminaivio dar
dalismaani haalimi via
via
via daali navi
nam namasmi avia
amoaani avi dar

BROKEN CAR

Brlj brlj brlj brlj brlj brlj
krakratrutra pruf
gungrula gungrula kakakakakaka
trachacha khrrrrrrrr

DREAMS GIVE REASON
TO OUR NIGHTS

www.ingramcontent.com/pod-product-compliance
Lightning Source LLC
Chambersburg PA
CBHW021011090426
42738CB00007B/751